Original title:
A Roadmap to Life (If You Can Read It)

Copyright © 2025 Creative Arts Management OÜ
All rights reserved.

Author: Charles Whitfield
ISBN HARDBACK: 978-1-80566-045-3
ISBN PAPERBACK: 978-1-80566-340-9

The Destination Unknown

I'm off to see the world, they say,
But I lost my map along the way.
With no GPS to guide my feet,
I just follow my nose for something sweet.

A signpost points with a silly grin,
I take a left, then a spin.
Where am I going? Who knows, dear friend,
Just hope there's snacks around the bend.

Reflections on Route

The rearview mirror shows me twice,
That missed turn back looked kinda nice.
I serenade the passing trees,
As they nod, saying, "Do as you please."

I stop for coffee, and a weird chat,
With a raccoon in a baseball hat.
He says, "Life's a ride, enjoy the fun,"
I laugh and say, "I'm the chosen one!"

The Landscape of Choices

Every fork's a puzzling quest,
Should I go left, or is right the best?
One road leads to a great buffet,
The other says, "Leave it for another day."

I flip a coin or maybe flip me,
Consequences are just a small fee.
With every choice, I've stirred the pot,
And hope that wisdom finds me a lot.

Streets Paved with Dreams

I walk these streets with my head held high,
Dodging raindrops that meander by.
The pavement's cracked but oh so bright,
With glittering hopes that light the night.

Each window holds a different tale,
Of quirky folks who never fail.
So if you stumble, just find your cheer,
Embrace the weirdness, hold it dear!

Guiding Stars

Bright lights overhead, a cosmic twist,
Navigating paths, they never miss.
Chasing dreams that zigzag far,
Hope you don't call a cat 'Noir.'

With every turn, a joke is made,
Detours taken, plans betrayed.
But laughter's guide will lead you well,
Through ups and downs, it casts a spell.

Mysterious Detours

Left or right, which way to go?
Maps all twisted, like a circus show.
A sandwich shop, that's hard to find,
Should've followed the squirrel, oh never mind!

An unplanned stop, a scenic spree,
Tourist traps and bees that flee.
Life's a maze with twists galore,
Just laugh it off and explore some more.

Where the Asphalt Ends

There's a sign that says, "Roadwork Ahead,"
But I'd prefer a comfy bed.
Grass grows wild, it shouts with glee,
Ever thought of taking a selfie with a tree?

Barefoot adventures, dirt on the heels,
Who knew life had such big appeals?
Somehow a puddle jumps in my way,
Splashes of laughter rule the day!

The Highway of Choices

Which flavor of ice cream will I take?
Peanut butter's good, but so is cake.
Each decision feels like a reel,
Maybe I'll just spin the wheel!

Winding roads lead to surprises galore,
Like dancing llamas outside a store.
Embrace the chaos, let it unfold,
Funny moments are the best kind of gold.

The Geography of Hope

In a land of dreams and snacks,
We navigate the quirky tracks.
With jellybeans to light the way,
And gumdrop clouds that never stay.

Surprise detours filled with cheer,
Magic signs that disappear.
A map that bends, and sometimes folds,
Where every twist is fun, not bold.

Crossroads of Possibility

At the forks of fate, we choose,
Will it be left, or right, or snooze?
Potholes filled with silly dreams,
And traffic lights that make us scream.

With each new path, a laugh we find,
Like misread signs that seem so blind.
A crosswalk painted polka dots,
Where every step is full of plots.

Mental Mile Markers

Counting miles on wrinkled maps,
Where logic takes some silly naps.
Each landmark cracked with tales to tell,
Like where I tripped and fell quite well.

With strange reminders on the ground,
And lost socks always making sound.
They lead me where I take a break,
To share a joke or slice of cake.

Threads of the Map

In threads of color, life we weave,
With tangled routes that none believe.
An X marks spots of joy and strife,
An accidental map of life.

With needle sharp, I stitch my way,
Through comic blunders every day.
Each loop a laugh, each knot a cheer,
As threads entwine to bring me near.

The Boundless Horizon Ahead

With snacks in my pocket and shoes untied,
I set out on a journey, my heart open wide.
The map is a doodle, ink smudged and unclear,
But who needs directions when adventure is near?

In a world full of loops and peculiar bends,
I laugh at my trips, my most loyal friends.
I chase after rainbows, they lead me astray,
But finding lost treasures makes it all play!

Compass Hearts and Wandering Souls

A compass that spins like a top on the loose,
Points north, then south, oh, what's the use?
With hearts full of wonder and shoes full of holes,
We dance on the map, with our wandering souls.

Each step is a giggle, each turn is a jest,
In the carnival of life, we're just guests.
So let's skip through the chaos, let laughter unfold,
Adventure is silly, but that's what we hold!

The Unmarked Trail of Questions

Why is the sky blue? Why don't cows fly?
The more that I ponder, the more minutes pass by.
With questions like breadcrumbs, I wander around,
But answers get lost, nowhere to be found.

On trails of confusion, I trip and I fall,
Each stumble a riddle, a curious call.
Yet joy is in finding the wonders we seek,
Amidst all the questions, it's laughter we speak!

Journey of Twists and Turns

The road is a serpent, it sways to and fro,
I'm dizzy with laughter, where shall I go?
With hiccups and giggles, I spin in a whirl,
Caught in the dizzy dance of this whimsical twirl.

Through twists that confound and turns that perplex,
I embrace the absurd, life's wild little specs.
So join me, dear friend, let the ride make us glee,
In this fun-filled excursion, we're truly carefree!

Blueprints of a Dreamer

In the land of silly schemes,
Where dreams are woven in bright seams,
I sketch my plans with crayon might,
Hoping they'll take off in flight.

I chart a course through ice cream lakes,
Past waffle forests and pancake flakes,
With gummy bears as trusty crew,
Together, we'll find something new.

My map's a mess of scribbled cheer,
With arrows facing every which sphere,
Yet somehow laughter guides my hand,
As I wander this whimsical land.

If you spot me lost in delight,
Just know I'm dancing with all my might,
Each step I take, a joke unfolds,
In the spirit of dreams that never grow old.

The Way Forward

I set out with a rubber band,
To stretch my fate and make a stand,
But somehow tripped on my own shoelace,
And now I'm in a wobbly race.

The signs I make are quite absurd,
"Turn left at the talking herd!"
With each misstep, I laugh away,
As life brings pranks in bright array.

My compass spins in dizzy loops,
Indicating marshmallow troops,
Yet still I march with goofy grace,
Embracing each detour I face.

So if you're searching for that road,
Remember laughter is the code,
Each bump I hit, a dance I sway,
Making joy my guiding way.

Unwritten

There once was a page, crisp and clean,
A spot for ideas yet unseen,
I doodled a cat, then a giant shoe,
Wondering what my life will do.

With squiggles and scribbles, I tried to find,
The way to mix silly with refined,
A roadmap drawn in jellybeans,
Leading to places no one has seen.

I wrote of times that I would glide,
On unicorns, with pizza as my guide,
Every laugh and giggle I've penned,
Turns a meandering path into a trend.

So grab your pen, let your heart sing,
Create your journey, take to wing,
For in the pages yet to unfold,
Lies a story that's merry and bold.

Constellations of Purpose

Stars above twinkle brightly,
Guiding the lost like a flashlight.
But really, don't trust them too much!
They lie sometimes, oh such a touch!

Maps in hand, we start our quest,
Finding our way, we jest and jest.
Each wrong turn's a laugh, don't you see?
Who knew getting lost could be so free?

The Scenic Route

Taking the long way seems so fun,
Driving in circles, oh what a run!
Pit stops for snacks, and some silly tunes,
Accidental detours under the moon.

We stop to smell every roadside flower,
Life's too short, so we linger an hour.
With laughter echoed beneath the sun,
Every mile's an adventure, everyone!

The Unmarked Trails

Off the path, we wander and roam,
Finding new joys far from home.
Each step we take, a giggle or two,
Who needs signposts? Not me, not you!

We stumble upon a quirky old shop,
With trinkets and treasures that make jaws drop.
In the chaos, we find a sweet sort of peace,
Life's unmarked trails are a puzzle, a piece.

Cartography of the Spirit

Drawing in sand with a twig or a pen,
Sketching our dreams, no map for where, when.
With lines that loop back like a spaghetti dish,
We twist and we turn, chasing a wish.

Clouds above throw shade on our plans,
But we'll dance in the rain, holding hands.
For every direction is one we can take,
Living our lives is the biggest mistake!

Signs Along the Way

Turn left at the sigh, right at the tune,
Watch for the shriek and the fainting raccoon.
Life's not a straight path, it's a twisty old game,
With markers of laughter and a dash of pure fame.

Don't mind the detours, embrace every bump,
Each sign tells a tale, like a life in a jump.
Watch out for potholes, and the roadkill brigade,
Just laugh at the chaos, making memories in spades.

Trailblazing Through Time

With sneakers that squeak on the cobblestone floor,
We chase down nostalgia, then beg for some more.
Tick-tock, dear watch, but slow down your spin,
As we race through the ages, just laugh at the din.

The fads come and go, like a flip-flop parade,
From bell-bottom pants to the tech that we've made.
Fashion advice? Please! It's merely a jest,
Mix stripes with polka dots, and call it your best!

The Compass Within

Your heart is the needle, it wiggles and sways,
It points to the joy in the most curious ways.
When lost in the woods or a marshmallow fight,
Just giggle and twirl, the stars will feel right.

Forget all the maps that are neatly displayed,
Follow the giggles, let your worries fade.
For every misstep, there's laughter in store,
With a ticklish heart, you'll always want more!

Footprints in the Sand

Slides, wobbles, and splats in our sandy delight,
Where footprints mix stories, each one feels just right.
You might trip on a shell, and land on your face,
But bubblegum moments just add to the grace.

The tide comes to dance, it erases the tale,
Yet memories linger, like the smell of fresh ale.
So strut with a grin, let the waves wash your fears,
For laughter is life's way to dry off our tears.

The Open Road to Tomorrow

With each twist and turn we find,
There's laughter and silliness intertwined.
Maps upside down, we're on a quest,
The compass spins, we take a rest.

Gas station coffee and snacks galore,
A treasure hunt at the local store.
We drive in circles just for the fun,
Who knew lost meant adventure begun?

Bumpy roads make our joy spring high,
With every wrong turn, we reach for the sky.
Silly stories spoken loud and clear,
Tomorrow's promise is always near.

So grab a snack and let's hit the road,
With jokes and laughter, lightening the load.
We may not know where the journey goes,
But with you, my friend, anything flows.

Enigmas of the Expedition

Puzzles pop up like mushrooms in spring,
Where do we go? Who's checking the wing?
With maps that giggle and signs that frown,
Our expedition feels like a clown's crown.

Navigating mysteries, we scratch our heads,
Eating hot dogs while dodging the spreads.
Each riddle solved brings a cheer,
Then we promptly forget where to steer.

Lost like socks in a laundry fight,
We dance on the edge of day and night.
Each detour leads us to splendid sights,
Who knew wanderlust sparked such delights?

Adventure awaits around every bend,
With laughter and friends, the rules we'll bend.
So let's embrace this silly caper,
For life is a map, with a hidden taper.

Roads Worn and Weathered

The path behind is full of tales,
Of wild storms, and happy trails.
We stumbled once, we stumbled twice,
But who knew failure could feel so nice?

Potholes like craters becoming our friends,
Every bump in the road, a message sends.
Adventures are better when taken in stride,
With rubber chickens perched on the side.

The sun is bright, the clouds are gray,
Who cares? We'll dance in our own way.
With donuts flying and laughter unfurled,
It's a worn-out road, but it suits our world.

Drive on, drive on, hilarious crew,
Worn shoes and maps all askew.
Each step taken with giggles and cheer,
The road isn't long when friends are near.

The Wayfarer's Wisdom

They say the road teaches lessons each mile,
But our GPS seems to be in denial.
It spins around like a merry-go-round,
Taking us nowhere, yet we're still bound.

A wise wayfarer laughs at the map,
"It's not about where, it's the fun in the gap."
With a wink and a grin, let's follow the stars,
To diners with pie and neon bars.

Mistakes lead us to unexpected feasts,
Like forgetting the cake for a birthday beast.
Yet joy found along the crooked way,
Is worth more than maps that lead us astray.

So gather your friends, let's all embrace,
The journey of life at a wild pace.
In laughter and joy, the wisdom lies,
Not in the route, but the laughter that flies.

Shadows and Sunlight

In the garden, plot twists bloom,
Where socks disappear, like a cartoon.
The sun shines bright, the shadows dance,
Life's a game, not left to chance.

Bananas wear peels, just for style,
The vases hold dust, all the while.
Coffee spills, a morning mess,
Laugh it off, we all confess.

Dogs chase tails, cats climb high,
A world that welcomes the silly sigh.
Wanderlust leads us, without a map,
Just follow the giggles, take a nap.

Rainy days bring puddles galore,
Jump in them all, who could ask for more?
Life's a circus, don't read the signs,
Just grab a friend, and share the vines.

The Atlas of Reflection

Maps are made of dreams, they say,
But mine's a pizza, by the way.
X marks the spot, with extra cheese,
A slice of life, oh pretty please!

Compass spins, dizzy but bold,
Following giggles, stories told.
Mirrors show faces, oh what a sight,
Laughing at time, what pure delight.

Paths meander like jokes shared loud,
Clouds look like elephants, oh so proud.
Scribbles on walls, the heart of the quest,
Every misstep, a jest at its best.

Treasure awaits in the mundane days,
Mismatched socks, in funny arrays.
Maps of laughter, on the floor,
Each step we take, opens a door.

In Search of North

Lost my compass, found the fun,
When looking for north, I spun and spun.
The sun said east, the moon said west,
But laughter's the only true quest.

Taking sidesteps, into a shop,
Where ice cream mountains, never stop.
Follow the giggles, not the stars,
Misguided bliss, in candy bars.

Phone maps are tricky, they lead to snacks,
While squirrels plot, in their secret packs.
Who knew detours led to delight,
Find this map in a single bite?

Shiny gadgets, missing directions,
Life's GPS? Just pure affections.
Chase the laughter, it'll guide you home,
In search of north, just laugh and roam.

Trails of Tomorrow

Tomorrow's trail, paved with dreams,
Full of chocolate and laughter screams.
With sprinkles of joy, bounce to the beat,
Life throws marbles, we move our feet.

Follow the path, where giggles ring,
Snakes with hats, and frogs that sing.
We'll ride on clouds, in marshmallow boats,
Navigate life like a pack of goats.

Tomorrow waits, with open arms,
Eager to share its quirky charms.
Grab your friends, and hold on tight,
To ride the waves of sheer delight.

Map the fun in every twist,
Forget the gloom, they don't exist.
Transforming trails, in joy we trust,
Forge ahead, in wonder we must.

Between the Lines of Life

Maps are drawn with crayons bright,
But which road is wrong, and which is right?
I followed a puppy, but he just ran,
Now I'm lost in a land of canned Spam.

With signs that point to Mystery Lane,
I honk and wave, but it's all in vain.
The GPS says to turn left and swirl,
I end up in a dance with a startled squirrel.

Detours dance like cats on the floor,
I can't remember what I'm searching for.
Each pit stop offers a slice of pie,
But if I eat more, I fear I might fly.

The road ahead is a silly sight,
With laughter echoing into the night.
So grab your hat and dance a jig,
Life's a wild ride, be sure to zig!

The Mapmaker's Heart

A mapmaker's heart goes a-twinkle,
With twists and turns that make you crinkle.
He scribbles paths with a wink and a grin,
Lost in the chaos, he finds joy within.

His compass spins like a top on ice,
Turn right at the cat, and now isn't that nice?
A vendor shouts, 'Get your road snacks here!'
I buy some gum and disappear in cheer.

His maps have hidden routes, oh so sly,
One led me to a disco with a karaoke guy.
I sang off-key, and folks gathered near,
Turns out my heart has no sense of fear!

In a world of lines, he draws with flair,
Making detours feel like a county fair.
Swing your partner, not a care in sight,
The mapmaker's heart glows like starlight!

Paths of Reflection

On paths of reflection, my shoe laces fight,
They trip me often, with glee so bright.
I stroll past puddles that wink and tease,
And whisper secrets on the warm breezes.

The signs say 'This Way' but point to the sky,
I ponder the wisdom of a passing fly.
In the mirror of water, my hair goes wild,
Who knew my reflection could look so beguiled?

I once took a turn by a tree made of cheese,
Fell in love with a squirrel who giggled with ease.
He offered me friendship, with acorns to share,
Together we plotted how to dance with a bear!

Paths converge, diverge, all in good fun,
Every twist, bend, echoes laughter, not done.
So here's to the journeys that make us sing,
On paths of reflection, let's see what life brings!

Footprints in Always Moving Sands

Footprints in sands that dance with the tide,
The beach is a canvas, my worries abide.
I build a sandcastle, it giggles with glee,
But the tide rolls in and says, 'You can't keep me!'

A crab named Larry wears a little crown,
He scrolls on the shore like a tiny clown.
With a wave of his claw, he calls me to play,
In a kingdom where footprints fade away.

The sun is a painter, splashing gold,
Each grain of sand, a story untold.
I dance on the shoreline, my footprints erased,
But the laughter we share can't ever be paced.

So next time you wander and feel like a fool,
Remember the sands and their slippery rule.
Jump in with joy, let loose all those plans,
Life's a wild adventure where laughter expands!

The Highways of the Heart

On this highway, emotions collide,
GPS says 'turn left', but I took a ride.
Traffic jams cause a funny twist,
And I completely forgot my list.

Road signs point, yet still I roam,
As I laugh and make silly poems.
Gas stations sell snacks, what a treat,
But only if I can find my seat.

Songs on the radio, lyrics unclear,
Chasing my dreams while munching on gear.
With friends all around, what a delight,
We're lost together, but it feels just right.

The Journey Without End

Where do we go? Who even knows?
We're on a train that never slows.
With every stop, a new surprise,
A clown on a bike, oh my, how time flies!

Passengers laugh as they share their tales,
While I try to check if my phone derails.
The snacks are endless, far too many,
And I can't find a seat, oh it's uncanny!

Round and round, we spin like tops,
As we gather memories, each one pops.
A journey of laughter, glee, and cheer,
With every detour, I hold them near.

Navigating Through Shadows

In the dark, I hold my map,
But it's upside down, what a mishap!
Shadows chuckle, they play a game,
I trip over roots—oh what a shame!

Lanterns flicker, trying to guide,
But I just laugh and take it in stride.
Ghosts share secrets of routes less known,
As I fumble and weave, feeling overthrown.

Yet in the dark, there's a glow of fun,
With each twist and turn, my spirit runs.
Shadows become friends, they teach me to play,
As we dance through the night, come what may.

Signposts of Self-Discovery

Stop here, it says, 'Find who you are,'
But my reflection looks quite bizarre.
With a silly grin and mismatched socks,
    Self-discovery feels like paradox!

Each signpost points to places unknown,
I took a detour where wildflowers grown.
They whispered softly, "Take your time,"
While squirrels danced to a silly rhyme.

I learned to stumble, giggle, and fall,
  Embrace the chaos, answer the call.
  Life's a circus, come join the show,
In this grand adventure, let laughter flow.

The Itinerary of Heartbeats

My heart made a list for today,
With coffee and donuts, hooray!
But then came the cat,
Who sat on the mat,
And disrupted my plans in a play.

A detour through laughter and cheer,
With friends who are always quite near.
We trip on our shoes,
Laugh off the blues,
And dance like nobody's here.

An amendment to routes must be made,
When traffic of thoughts starts to invade.
We zig and we zag,
With a laugh and a brag,
For fun is the joy we've displayed.

Rolling forward to tomorrow's delight,
With hopes that take flight in the night.
So grab that ice cream,
And live out the dream,
In this silly itinerary, all right!

Unfolding Maps of Tomorrow

With crayons, we sketch a grand plan,
But life is a mischievous man.
Paths twist and they turn,
And we try not to burn,
While missing the bus for a tan.

We bravely navigate all our years,
Through laughter and sometimes through tears.
With GPS wrong,
We sing silly songs,
Adjusting our sights and our gears.

Tomorrow awaits, full of fun,
With dreams that are never quite done.
We'll ride on a bike,
Or hitchhike a hike,
While chasing the rays of the sun.

So fold up the map, let it go,
For life's a wild, whimsical show.
With snacks on our way,
And banter to sway,
Tomorrow we might just find flow!

Cartography of Choices

Choices are paths that we take,
Like picking a cake or a shake.
Do I want it round?
Or maybe the sound
Of chocolate, which makes my heart quake?

A fork in the road turns to pie,
With flavors that catch my sly eye.
One bites, then they dive,
To see who survives,
The joy of sweet treats stacked high.

Directions can lead us astray,
With GPS sitting in dismay.
But turns that we choose,
Can seldom confuse,
When laughter is part of the play.

So chart out the course of your whim,
With giggles and light on a limb.
Each turn that you take,
Brings joy in the wake,
Of choices that sparkle and brim!

Waypoints in the Wilderness

In jungles of busy and loud,
We wander to find that sweet crowd.
With treasures we seek,
And maps that feel weak,
We giggle and stumble quite proud.

We pitch our tents under the stars,
And dream of big journeys by cars.
With marshmallows toasted,
And laughter coasted,
Our wild tales become cosmic memoirs.

Navigating through twists and bends,
With signs that make fun of our friends.
Each barrier crossed,
Nothing seems lost,
As we count all the joy that transcends.

So prance through the woods in delight,
Where laughter's the best guiding light.
With every wrong turn,
There's joy to discern,
In this wilderness wonder of might!

Echoes of the Road

I took a left at the rubber tree,
But found a sign, "No entry!"
A cow was dancing, wearing shoes,
Gave my GPS the blues.

The map was upside down, it seems,
My phone decided to take a nap,
So I followed a flock of screaming geese,
They led me to a funny trap.

With each wrong turn, I found a joke,
A llama offered me a smoke,
I laughed so hard, I missed my lane,
But who needs routes when you have gain?

At the end of it all, I found my way,
Chasing laughter through the fray,
Life's a ride, with twists and bends,
Just enjoy the ride, my friends!

The Path Less Traveled

I veered off course, my compass spun,
Found a sign that said 'Just for Fun.'
A parade of squirrels waved me by,
I joined the march, to my surprise.

The yellow brick road turned green with mold,
A pirate yelled, "Be brave, be bold!"
I traded my compass for a slice of pie,
"Who needs direction?" I asked with a sigh.

They say the road is paved with gold,
But mine's all rock, or so I'm told,
I tripped on laughs, fell down the cracks,
Made friends with a frog who gives good hacks.

So if you're lost, don't shed a tear,
Chase the jokes that bring you cheer,
For every step, a laugh or two,
Is better than following the cue!

Lost and Found in Transit

I packed my bags, left home in haste,
Forgot my map, such a big waste.
Found a sock that claimed to be a guide,
In a taxi that was my ride.

The driver turned up a nonsense tune,
"Socks can't drive, that's what I hold!"
We laughed and sped past every sign,
Each wrong way felt just so fine.

A street magician grinned, "Got a trick!,"
He made my route disappear quick.
But I didn't mind, I sang along,
Life's a stage, and I love this song!

At the bus stop, I met a cat,
Who told me tales and sat on my hat,
I realized then, while they all frown,
Getting lost means you'll never drown.

A Symphony of Directions

The map was scored like a piece of art,
But I lost the beat right from the start.
I zigged and zagged, a waltz of woe,
As car horns played, "Please just go slow!"

With arrows dancing on the road,
My left foot tapped to the wrong code.
An unexpected chorus of wrong turns,
Brought me laughter as my spirit burns.

I met a poet at an old red light,
Who recited rhymes and brought delight.
She said, "Dear friend, it's not the map,
But the fun you have that helps you clap!"

So let the traffic play its tune,
As I laugh along under the moon.
For in this chaos, I find my way,
Just follow the fun, come what may!

Cartography of the Mind

In the city of thoughts, I roam,
Searching for routes to call my home.
Each signpost giggles, with arrows askew,
Maps that lead to coffee, not true love, too.

Streets paved with wishes and dreams surreal,
Where GPS is often an unruly wheel.
Every detour leads to a quaint little shop,
With pastries that whisper, 'Just one more stop!'

Navigating moments, I trip and I fall,
A genius of chaos, I'm having a ball.
Each twist and turn brings laughter anew,
On this quirky journey, my wits will ensue.

So if you feel lost, don't worry, my friend,
Follow the silly paths, around each bend.
Life's not a puzzle, but a cheeky jest,
Chase the bright signs, and let humor be best.

The Drift of Events

Life's a river, with bends and spins,
Where plans go belly up, and chaos begins.
I packed my lunch, but forgot a fork,
Eating with fingers, my effective work.

Events like balloons, float here and there,
Some pop with laughter, others with flair.
I wake up early, just to sleep in,
Chasing my tail, let the games begin!

Every day's a twist, like a dance in the rain,
Juggling my tasks, but mostly in vain.
I signed up for yoga, lost my last shoe,
Did a headstand, oh what a view!

Events keep drifting, like leaves on a breeze,
I'll ride this wave, or fall to my knees.
With humor as compass, I journey along,
Laughing at life, where I truly belong.

Orbits of Encounter

Around and around, we spin through the day,
Meeting odd characters who come out to play.
A neighbor who sings, but flat as a note,
And dogs that conspire, on a rescue boat.

I bump into friends at the strangest of hours,
Under the influence of freshly bloomed flowers.
Each chat a comet, bursting like pop,
As we muse on the moon, and all its flip-flops.

With cosmic collisions of laughter and fun,
We'll orbit each other 'til our time's done.
Sharing our tales, with tea and delight,
In this galaxy of moments, we shine so bright.

So steer your spaceship to where joy is found,
In the orbits of friends, laughter knows no bounds.
Let the stars be our guide, on paths we create,
In a universe bizarre, we choose to celebrate.

The Journey of Many Steps

Each step a giggle, each mile a song,
Through stumbling valleys where we all belong.
With shoes untied, I skip down the lane,
Collecting lost socks, it's part of the game.

The road gets wobbly, but I don't despair,
I'll hop, skip, jump—just breathing the air.
A bird dive-bombs, and I duck with a spin,
Finding joy in the chaos, oh what a win!

I pass by a booth selling dreams on a stick,
The flavors of life—both savory and slick.
With every odd turn, a story takes shape,
In the murals of minutes, we twist and reshape.

So join in my journey, it's wild and it's weird,
With laughter as fuel, I'll persevere.
For in every misstep, a treasure there lies,
Life's dance is perplexing, yet oh so wise.

The Byways of Being

In the land of socks and mismatched shoes,
We wander through options, left to choose.
Where the coffee's hot, yet the cups are cold,
And tales of wild travel begin to unfold.

GPS says right, but left feels more fun,
Turned round and around, but hey, we've just begun.
With snacks in the back and tunes all around,
Life's rolling on wheels, and laughter is found.

For every slight detour, there's silliness gained,
A misplaced map leads to joy, uncontained.
We dance in the rain, or slip on the wet,
With each little twist, new surprises we get.

So here's to life's twists, those quirky little paths,
Where pitfalls are laughter and sarcasm laughs.
The journey's the punchline, the ride's not a test,
With giggles in tow, we're truly the best.

The Journey's Latitude

On a day full of snacks, and a map upside down,
The compass is dizzy, but we wear the crown.
With every misstep, there's joy in the mess,
Navigating life's chaos can't be a stress.

We stop at the diner for pancakes galore,
As syrup drips endlessly, we beg for more.
Our steering wheel dances as we sing along,
With every wrong turn, we find where we belong.

The horizon is goofy, like a funhouse mirror,
Where distances shrink and reality's clearer.
With giggles as fuel, and laughter our guide,
Each straying heartbeat becomes our wild ride.

So here's to the latitude, varying and free,
Where there's no need to stress about "where should we be?"
For every odd ending's a start cleverly spun,
In this silly adventure, we've won—oh, what fun!

Markers of Meaning

Each sign tells a story, like an old friend's joke,
Get lost on purpose; you might find a bloke.
A whale of a tale or a cloud shaped like fries,
Life's markers of meaning are puppets in disguise.

We follow the breadcrumbs, they lead us to pies,
Who knew breadcrumbs could wear such delicious ties?
Caution: slippery slopes where the giggles might flow,
Jumping puddles of wisdom, oh, where will we go?

With every red light, a moment to pause,
To laugh at the sun or explore life's applause.
No urgency here, just a playful parade,
As we waltz with our dreams—together, unscayed.

So heed the odd markers, those silly old signs,
For laughter, my friend, is where life truly shines.
Embrace each odd turn, relish life's charms,
And dance with the moments—come hug me in arms!

Unfolding the Path Ahead

Imagine a journey that's silly and sweet,
With sneakers to stroll and a warm, friendly seat.
A kite in the sky, all tangled and bright,
Unfolding our stories in pure morning light.

With ice cream for breakfast and rainbows for snacks,
We wander through mischief in soft, silly tracks.
Each puddle's a splash zone, each giggle a boost,
In the wild garden of life, we happily roost.

A signpost reads 'wrong way'—the humor it brings,
Like getting lost means we're hunting for wings.
Through paths overrun where the wildflowers grow,
We dance to the rhythm our spirits bestow.

So here's to the moments that twist and expand,
Where laughter and sunshine go hand in hand.
For every step forward, there's joy to be bled,
In this whimsical journey, the fun lies ahead!

Journeying Through Uncharted Paths

In a land where llamas dance,
I tripped over a tree branch glance.
A sign said 'this way' with a wink,
But all I found was a missing link.

With hiking boots that squeak and squeal,
I pondered how to make my next meal.
A map that folds like a taco shell,
Points to a place I can't quite spell.

I met a squirrel with great advice,
He said, 'Just follow the road that's nice.'
But which road's nice? I don't quite know,
So I just danced in the grass and fro.

The sun went down, the stars took flight,
I finally figured I'm not too bright.
Yet laughter leads me on this quest,
In the end, it's all just a hilarious test.

The Compass of Dreams

My compass spins like a top of fun,
Pointing east, west, 'round, and done.
Is that my dream or a pizza slice?
With toppings galore, now isn't that nice?

I chased a cloud that looked like a cat,
Swirling round in a cozy hat.
It meowed directions, but where to go?
I ended up in a muddy stow.

The stars above seem to giggle and jest,
With dreams that swirl like a wobbly fest.
But laughter's my guide, come rain or shine,
Even in chaos, all things align.

A whimsical ride, this life of mine,
Though I must admit, the turns entwine.
With a smile on my face, I'll flow with the stream,
After all, who needs a perfect dream?

Navigating the Maze of Existence

I wandered through a maze of cheese,
With rats who laughed and danced with ease.
One whispered, 'Left, then a right, oh dear!'
But I found myself back at the root beer.

Every turn stole a slice of my grin,
As I stumbled through this cheddar din.
A goat with glasses offered a map,
Said, 'Follow the smell—I'm taking a nap!'

Navigating life's twists can be tricky,
Like finding the punchline in a bad flicky.
A detour here leads to a party of mice,
Now that's a place that sounds pretty nice!

So if you go and hit a wall,
Just have a giggle and give it your all.
For in the maze that goes round and round,
Laughter, my friend, is life's best sound.

Directions in the Dust

I scribbled paths on a dusty page,
And somehow found a clever sage.
He merely chuckled and waved his hand,
And got lost while trying to make a stand.

The wind blew strong, my plans took flight,
As I chased after shadows in the night.
Every footprint led to a giggling brook,
In a book where no one cares how to look.

My map is a doodle, my compass awry,
Yet every detour makes me ask why.
With a sprinkle of joy and a dash of cheer,
I dance through uncertainties without fear.

So here's to mishaps and laughter, dear friend,
In a world that rolls on, let's pretend.
For every wrong turn is just a new start,
In this funny journey straight from the heart.

Histories in the Dust

In the attic, ghosts of shoes,
Left behind with all the blues.
Maps that lie, filled with dreams,
Shiny paths and broken beams.

Spilled coffee on my big plan,
Jumbled pages, such a jam.
Where to turn, left or right?
Life's confusion, a silly sight.

I once tried to find my way,
Used a cat to save the day.
It led me straight to the fridge,
Now I sit, it's my own bridge.

Every corner holds a laugh,
Directions drawn in doodled graph.
Forget the path, let's have some fun,
Step back and soak up the sun.

The Guidebook of Experiences

With pages torn and edges frayed,
Life's advice is poorly laid.
Read the guide, then flip it fast,
Wonder how the time flew past.

I asked a frog for some tips,
It only croaked and made me trip.
The wisdom hid beneath a rock,
Turns out he just loved to mock.

Each page a tale of bliss or woe,
Throw it away, let the chaos flow.
Dancing wildly, I lose the plot,
Who needs a guide? Not me, I thought!

So here I stand with dreams in hand,
Life's nonsense, I make a stand.
When plans go wrong, remember this:
It's all just part of joyful bliss.

Expo in the Rain

Umbrellas up, we dance around,
Life's expo, splashes abound.
Leaky tents and bright ideas,
We pitch our dreams with goofy cheers.

Map got soggy, bends and tears,
Try to navigate through all my fears.
The food truck's line could take all day,
But pizza's worth the long delay.

Oh look, a booth for ancient scams,
Offering wisdom from old ham.
Advice so stale, yet we still grin,
Finding laughter where we begin.

Drenched but happy, we twirl and spin,
In the rain, we lose, but also win.
With every drop, a chuckle shared,
This zany life, no one prepared!

Balancing the Compass

A compass spins, it breaks the mold,
Points are flipped; the map is old.
North or south? Who really knows?
I'll follow squirrels wherever they go.

Guide me, oh unsteady hand,
Through uncharted, wobbly land.
Even Google Maps has lied,
Leading me to nowhere wide.

A tightrope walk on life's thin line,
Juggling dreams over a glass of wine.
If I tip, I'll just laugh it off,
Join in the fun, no time for scoff.

So here's my tip for anyone lost,
Embrace the chaos, count the cost.
In life's odd dance, let humor reign,
We'll find our way through joy and pain.

Navigating Dreams

In a land of sleep, the maps are drawn,
With signs that wink, and paths that yawn.
I take a left, where dreams collide,
Only to find a giant slide.

Unicorns guide with glittery glee,
As I hunt for treasure beneath a tree.
But all I find is candy and gobs,
A sticky mess that's full of sobs.

Frogs in bow ties give me odd looks,
As I try to read from enchanted books.
I mix my paths, I twist and twirl,
In this silly land where dreams unfurl.

Yet laughter echoes through the skies,
With each wrong turn, a sweet surprise.
So I skip along, with joy and zest,
In this dreamland's quest, I'm truly blessed.

Uncharted Paths

With a compass that spins and a map that's torn,
I venture forth, a traveler reborn.
The forest smiles, the trees wave hello,
I trip on roots, putting on quite the show.

A path made of marshmallows leads me astray,
But I'll munch my way through, come what may.
The squirrels critique my navigator skills,
As I dodge acorns and tumble down hills.

Through waterfalls dancing, I slip and slide,
While dancing bears join in my joyride.
Who needs a plan? I'll just follow the beat,
Of life's crazy rhythm, oh, what a treat!

In laughter and mishaps, I find my way,
The uncharted paths lead to brighter days.
So here's to the wild, the absurd, the fun,
In this game of life, I've already won!

The Map of Our Journeys

If life had a map with bright neon lights,
Would it lead to pizza or magical sights?
Directions so vague, I'm lost on page two,
Looping in circles, what's a person to do?

A fork in the road, where should I go?
One way to gold, the other to a show.
I toss a coin, it bounces and spins,
Turns out it leads to where the fun begins!

At crossroads of laughter, I pause and I think,
Should I chase rainbows or dance by the sink?
With whimsical signs that flip and that flop,
I choose to embrace the whimsical hop.

So here's to our journeys, both silly and bold,
With maps made of giggles and stories retold.
In the twists and turns, we'll find our delight,
Creating our paths, with nothing but light!

Directions to Destiny

Grab your GPS, but make it a joke,
It says, 'Turn right at the nearest bloke.'
I follow directions that twist and that bend,
Finding treasure maps made of noodle and blend.

Through valleys of whimsy, I bounce and I prance,
With gummy bears singing, I join in their dance.
But beware of the trolls, oh they're having a ball,
With riddles and giggles; they'll try to enthrall!

The signs are all jumbled, a mishmash of cheer,
Reversing my steps, I'm close—oh so near!
An arrow that points to uncharted delight,
With each cracked-up laugh, my spirit takes flight.

So off to my destiny—I take a deep breath,
Embracing each folly, I'll dance past all the rest.
For life is a journey, a ha-ha parade,
In the book of my heart, the best plans are made!

Scribbles on a Sunset Sky

Crayons lost in golden hue,
Drawing futures, just for you.
A map that giggles, sings, and sways,
With arrows pointing all the ways.

Wobbly lines that twist and turn,
Missing spots, oh how we yearn!
But laughter guides the chosen path,
Who needs a plan when you can math?

Clouds might spill and flip around,
Puddles form beneath the ground.
Each splash a step, oh what a blast,
A scribbled journey, unsurpassed!

So grab your pen and doodle near,
Sketch your dreams without a fear.
The sunset's wild, a playful sight,
Your road to joy, oh what a flight!

Guiding Stars in Twilight

Stars that giggle twinkling high,
Pointing out where dreams can fly.
A compass made of jokes and cheer,
To find the fun that brought you here.

Constellations, funky shapes,
Guiding dreams like candy grapes.
They whisper secrets in the night,
When you feel lost, they're your light.

Don't fret if paths feel far away,
Just follow laughs, and you'll be gay.
Silly signs will keep you bold,
Adventure waits, or so I'm told!

So spin around and dance a bit,
Let the stars decide your wit.
In twilight's glow, come share your glee,
Life's route's a puzzle, wait and see!

The Route to Rediscovery

Finding paths through silly bends,
With rubber maps and quirky trends.
Detours lead to ice cream shops,
And maybe take us to the tops.

Lost your keys? Just stop and laugh,
Maybe they're a part of the path.
A wiggly route to rediscover,
The joy in every hidden cover.

Each wrong turn a door to chuckles,
Life's simply filled with joyful struggles.
Grab that compass, toss the guide,
Wander freely, don't just hide!

So scribble notes on every page,
In this wild, delightful stage.
Rediscover who you are, my friend,
With laughter as your faithful blend!

Navigating Through Clouds of Uncertainty

Clouds are fluff, and winds are wild,
Chasing dreams just like a child.
A foggy map? We'll make it clear,
With giggles that can outshine fear.

Stumbling through the misty maze,
Finding joy in quirky ways.
A detour here—and trip and fall,
But laughter echoes through it all.

So let's get lost, embrace the fun,
You cannot miss what's just begun.
Each twist a chance to dance about,
Navigating with joyous shout.

So take a breath, let worries cease,
In cloudy skies, we'll find our peace.
Your journey's bright, so don't you fret,
Clouds can't hide fun you'll never forget!

The Terrain of Time

In the valley of the past, we trip,
On memories sticky like a chip.
Time's a winding twisty lane,
With detours marked by joy and pain.

We climb the peaks of hopes and dreams,
But often find they burst at seams.
A slip and slide, oh what a sight,
As we navigate through day and night.

A map that's scribbled, hard to read,
With every turn, we plant a seed.
Lost in laughter, found by tears,
Our journey dances through the years.

The road seems short, or maybe long,
With silly signs that sing a song.
Let's keep on driving, full of cheer,
The fun is in the mess, my dear!

Budgeting Breath and Miles

Gas prices rise like a panicked balloon,
We budget our breath like a chef with a spoon.
Every mile costs more than we thought,
But laughter's free, or so I was taught.

The snacks take the biggest slice of the pie,
With chips and soda stacked up high.
Counting calories while burning gas,
Who knew life was such a funny class?

The odometer spins like a top,
As we chase the dreams that never stop.
Roadside diners with the quirkiest names,
Serve laughter alongside their strange games.

We'll economize joy; that budget's a joke,
As we roll with the punches and laugh till we choke.
Each pit stop is gluttony, oh what a thrill,
Life's a funny car ride on a budgeted bill!

Notes from the Roadside

Oh, roadside signs that catch the eye,
With slogans silly enough to fly.
"Free hugs ahead," "Turn back now,"
Navigating life like some weird cow.

With tires that squeal and music loud,
We blast through memories; oh, the crowd!
A detour here, a stop for ice cream,
Life's a river, flowing with a dream.

Sticky notes plastered on our dash,
"Don't forget to laugh," funky and brash.
We scribble our thoughts like a mad poet,
In this strange trip, we just can't blow it.

So here's to the moments that make us grin,
The unexpected stops, the wild spin.
We'll treasure each note, and when we arrive,
We'll look back and giggle, feeling alive!

The Kite in the Sky

A kite soars high on a windy day,
Tangled in clouds, it sways to play.
With a tail so long, it flicks and flies,
Chasing the dreams that dance in the skies.

We launch our hopes with a hearty scream,
To see how far they stretch and beam.
But sometimes it twists, and it takes a dive,
Reminding us all just to survive.

"It's just a string!" we laugh and shout,
As we run along, round and about.
When life gets caught in a snare or twine,
We untangle the mess, and all is fine.

So hold that string, let the winds decide,
In this funny ride, we all take pride.
A twist, a turn, oh what a flight,
Life's a kite, soaring in the light!

Waypoints of Wisdom

If you find a fork, take a snack,
Better than a map, that's a fact.
Turn left for coffee, the right for tea,
No one's lost if they're happy, you see.

Maps can be funny, full of squiggles,
With every twist, the laughter giggles.
A detour may lead to places unknown,
Like a café that serves your favorite scone.

Count the cows as they casually stroll,
One for the money, and two for the roll.
When in doubt, just follow the lane,
Every wrong turn can lead to more gain.

Ink on the paper? Oh, what a mess!
Doodles of dreams, it's anyone's guess.
Embrace the chaos, just take a ride,
With your trusty snacks, what a wild side!

The Journey Unfolds

Pack a sandwich, grab a drink,
Life's a picnic, don't overthink.
With every bend, laughter will grow,
Even when the GPS says no-go.

Lost your way? That's part of the game,
Endless stories, never the same.
Find the humor in every wrong turn,
Lessons are sprinkled; it's wisdom you learn.

Clouds might gather, don't lose your cheer,
Dance in the rain; the end is still near.
With friends by your side, you'll always thrive,
Road trips are joy rides, we're all alive.

Maps might fade, but memories stay,
Like funny moments we lived every day.
Take a picture—it lasts forever,
The journey's the treasure, oh, how clever!

A Cartographer's Heart

With paper and pen, I sketch my view,
A puzzle of places, where the wild things grew.
X marks the spot? Just a joke, you see,
It's all about the people, and their glee.

Drawn lines hide treasures, oh what a thrill,
From giant donuts to that big blue hill.
Funny how paths twist and suddenly wind,
Every step's a giggle waiting to find.

The compass spins, what a playful trick,
Just follow the laughter; it'll do the trick.
Maps may be guidelines, but words we'll rhyme,
In the art of wandering, we'll have a good time.

So throw out your maps, give a wink and cheer,
Adventure awaits—come on, my dear!
With every heartbeat, we chart our course,
In the land of the joyous, we find our force.

Routes of Reflection

Dirt roads twist like a great old story,
Full of mishaps, laughter, and little bit worrying.
Every bump is a giggle, a chance to sing,
The ride itself is a fabulous fling.

With sun on your face, and wind in your hair,
Life's too short for the straight and the fair.
Follow the rabbit if you wish to roam,
Through fields of daisies, you'll find your home.

Turn down side streets, be brave and bold,
Collect all the memories, more precious than gold.
Can't read the signs? Just make up your own,
In this wacky world, you're never alone.

So come join the fun, let's lose track of time,
With laughter as fuel, every road will rhyme.
Maps might be rough, but here's the truth,
The best routes are those that light up your youth!

The Art of Getting Lost

Wandered off the beaten path,
Stumbled on a spelling math.
Turns out 'wrong' can mean 'right',
Who knew getting lost was quite a sight?

Maps with squiggles, curious lines,
Lost some time but found some wines.
Uncharted areas, full of mirth,
Maybe getting lost is a new rebirth.

Left the compass back at home,
Following a cat, now I roam.
Through gardens, alleys, and a maze,
Turns out I'm here to soak up rays.

So here's a toast to the delight,
In wandering blind and out of sight.
Life's a trip with twists and bends,
And being lost? That's how it ends!

Signposts of the Soul

A signpost says, 'Go left, my friend',
But right looks good—I just pretend.
Tangled up in thoughts profound,
What sign was that? I'm glory-bound!

"If lost, stop, think, and reflect!"
So I stop for snacks, what did you expect?
A healthy choice—how heroic—
Chips and soda? Yep, that's my story, yo!

Every marker leads to stories tall,
'Watch for bears!' They laugh, then brawl.
I'm just hoping for a nice cold drink,
But at least my soul is set to think.

Go laugh with me, take a stroll,
In riddles, questions, they take their toll.
But in this life, let's take the cue:
Signposts of joy—here's to me and you!

Steps on a Fateful Journey

I took a step, then tripped, oh dear,
On my shoelace tied in cheer.
Rolling down a hill like a ball,
Thank goodness the grass caught my fall!

Next to the sign that's falling apart,
Waiting for wisdom to just start.
Step one: Don't step in that puddle!
But here I go—oh, what a muddle!

With each footprint marking my trail,
I dance along, I will not fail.
Gravity's a friend I tease,
I'll hop and skip with perfect ease.

So here's to swift steps, sometimes clumsy,
Life is better when it's bumpy.
Each journey's wild with giggles and glee,
I'll step my way through history!

The Road Less Traveled

There's a fork in the road, they said to me,
I took the one that smelled like brie.
Spicy trails, a cheese lover's dream,
Who knew a journey could be this creamy?

With paths entwining like spaghetti noodles,
I lead my life like free-range poodles.
Twists and turns, it's all absurd,
Lost my phone but found a bird.

Each step away from the normal grind,
Had me pondering what I might find.
Wacky creatures, nonsense galore,
It's hard to keep my spirits low, that's for sure!

So as I wander with smile and flair,
I embrace the quirks that hang in the air.
In this life, it's the laughs that matter,
Taking the road that thumps and clatters!

The Map that Leads Home

With arrows pointin' left and right,
I chose the road less bright.
The compass spins like a top,
I hope I don't fall and drop.

My lunch is now a mystery,
The squirrels hold my history.
Maps say all roads should lead,
Yet here I am, lost indeed.

I stop and ask a chatty tree,
"Can you direct this fool to me?"
The branch just shakes its leafy head,
And I grumble as I tread.

But then a stranger shows a smile,
With antics that are worth the while.
Together we map out a plan,
Who knew life was so grand?

A Tapestry of Trails

There's a path that zigzags funny,
Leading to a spot with honey.
Each turn is quite absurd,
Who knew trees could hum a word?

A cactus waves as I pass by,
"Do you want to give it a try?"
I laugh and grab a prickly snack,
Oh, now I need a real plan to track.

A waterfall spills like my drink,
I stop to pause and really think.
Are these signs or just mirages?
Maybe this is a game of carriages.

But at the end, what do I see?
A sign that reads, "Just be free!"
With laughter echoing in the air,
It seems the journey's made of flair.

Journeying Through Seasons

In spring, I took a little stroll,
Tripped on flowers, lost control.
Bunny rabbits laughed out loud,
I fell into a stinky cloud.

Summer sun blazed bright and bold,
Found a map scribbled in gold.
But it led straight to the beach,
Where ice-cream cones were within reach.

Come fall, the leaves turn crispy,
I chased a squirrel, oh, so frisky.
He swiped my hat without a care,
Then giggled as I pulled my hair.

In winter's chill, I slipped and slid,
On icy paths, my map they hid.
But laughter warmed my frosty toes,
In this journey, joy overflows.

Pathways to the Soul

Each path I take is full of cheer,
With wobbly signs that disappear.
My shoes are mismatched, so what's the fuss?
Adventure calls, it's a must!

I met a cat wearing a hat,
Said, "Follow me, we'll have a chat."
She led me to a café high,
Where sugar clouds floated by.

With every detour I embrace,
I find my smile in every place.
Lost and found, what a delightful tale,
Life's a circus, I'm on the trail.

The signs may crack and wane away,
But laughter guides my bumbling way.
At last, I see the sun ignite,
My heart, my map, that's pure delight.

The Trail of Epiphanies

In the forest of thought, I lost my way,
The trees whispered secrets that led me astray.
A squirrel gave guidance with a flick of its tail,
I followed its path, through sunshine and hail.

Each step a delight, with laughter to share,
Stumbling on wisdom, floating in air.
The answers were silly, like socks on a goat,
And who knew enlightenment came with a coat?

I danced with a rabbit, hummed tunes with a bee,
They chuckled and nodded; "Just trust and be free!"
So I scribbled my thoughts on a leaf with a pen,
A roadmap to nonsense, again and again.

And though I was lost, my heart felt so light,
With each funny twist, the future seemed bright.
So if you feel stuck, just follow the fun,
For life's silly trail has only begun!

Paved Paths and Detours

I woke up one morning, the sun in my eye,
And thought, "Today's the day, I'll reach for the sky!"
But tripping on flip-flops, I fell with a thud,
A detour emerged, from my plan made of mud.

The signposts were wobbly, and so was my brain,
With arrows pointing sideways, the town looked insane.
I waved to a chicken, who clucked with delight,
Said, "Follow my lead, it'll be quite a sight!"

Detours turned into adventures galore,
With ice cream for breakfast and naps on the floor.
Each twist was a giggle, each turn was a prank,
Life's routes are more fun when you dance on the plank.

So here's to the paths that lead us astray,
To laughter and mischief that colors our day.
When the road gets ridiculous, let out a cheer,
For every kooky turn brings joy that is near!

Streets of Serendipity

On a street named Surprise, I found a lost shoe,
It seemed so out of place, like a cow in a zoo.
I picked it up gently, gave it a spin,
And met a lost kitten, with mischief to win.

Together we wandered down paths filled with quirks,
Finding pizza-flavored clouds and dancing with jerks.
We rode on a bicycle that played jazz with flair,
And waltzed with the mailman, without any care.

The streetlights were giggling, the pavement was sly,
I stopped for a snack, ate a slice of the sky.
As we painted our dreams on the canvas of night,
This crazy excursion felt perfectly right.

So venture on streets that twist and confound,
Embrace every bump, let joy know no bound.
For the treasures you find in life's silly spree,
Are the gems of delight that are meant to be free!

Echoes of the Unknown Journey

In echoes of laughter, I set off at dawn,
With a short little tune and a very tall con.
The path was a riddle, a puzzle of fun,
With whispers from shadows, and jokes by the sun.

I tripped over wisdom and danced with surprise,
While ducks in bow ties debated the skies.
The trees held their breath, and giggled away,
Sharing tales of the strange as I wandered astray.

I chased after rainbows that led to a shop,
Where dreams were for sale, and giggles don't stop.
With each silly option, I spun and I twirled,
Collecting the nonsense that brightened my world.

So if you hear echoes, just follow them near,
For the journey's the treasure, and laughter is clear.
In the fun of the unknown, life's magic awaits,
With giggles and joys that unlock all the gates!

www.ingramcontent.com/pod-product-compliance
Lightning Source LLC
Chambersburg PA
CBHW051641160426
43209CB00004B/750